MUSICIANS INSTITUTE

T0053074

PRIVATE LESSONS

Essential
RHYTHM GUITAR

PATTERNS, PROGRESSIONS, AND TECHNIQUES FOR ALL STYLES

by Steve Trovato

ISBN 978-0-7935-8154-2

HAL•LEONARD®
CORPORATION

7777 W. BLUEMOUND RD. P.O. BOX 13819 MILWAUKEE, WI 53213

Visit Hal Leonard Online at
www.halleonard.com

Contents

Introduction

This book is based on the concept that, for most popular music styles, there exist a few basic, fundamental rhythm guitar techniques and a set of appropriate chords and chord voicings that determine the sound of each style.

Contained herein are *seven* popular musical guitar styles: country, fingerstyle acoustic, blues, rock, Latin and Brazilian, swing and jazz, and funk. For each one, I have written several progressions typical of that style. Included in each section are stylistically typical chord voicings, rhythms, and basic strum or accompaniment patterns. Each section also includes variations of the basic pattern that are progressively more challenging.

I hope that you will be able to use these stylistic concepts and apply them to the chord progressions of your favorite songs, to accompany yourself or another person, or to perform as rhythm guitar player in a band.

—*Steve Trovato*

Chapter **1** Country

Most country music is based around a straight eighth-note feel and makes extensive use of "cowboy chords"—open-position chord voicings. This gives the music a pure and simple quality. It also enables you to grab chords more quickly and not have to look at the guitar neck, in the event that you're a singer and are accompanying yourself.

The feel of country is produced by playing alternating bass notes. Usually, these will be the root (or tonic) and the fifth of whatever chords are being played. These bass notes are played on beats 1 and 3 of each measure, and a chord strum is then played on beats 2 and 4. This gives a pendulum-like, back-and-forth motion to the accompaniment.

Alternating Bass

Fig. 1 is our most basic rhythm. To play it, simply pick single notes on beats 1 and 3, and then strum downward and play the higher notes in each chord on beats 2 and 4. To produce the best sound, use downstrokes exclusively.

Notice the use of open-position chords. This progression begins in the key of G major and then moves to the key of E minor. Notice that the chords (except for the B7) are either major or minor without the addition of the 7th degree.

1 ▸ **Fig. 1**

Variation 1—Hammer-Ons

Fig. 2 uses the same chord progression as Fig. 1, but introduces hammer-ons to give more of a bluegrass sound. A *hammer-on* is produced by first playing the grace note (small one) and then striking the string hard enough with your fretting hand finger to produce a sound at the fret desired. This may take some practice, but the results will be well worth the effort.

Once again, use only downstrokes with your picking hand.

Fig. 2

Variation 2—Double Strumming

Fig. 3 is once again identical to both Figs. 1 and 2—your fretting hand will play the exact same chords and hammer-ons—but now we have a slightly different strumming pattern in the right hand. The steady downstrokes on beats 2 and 4 will be replaced by a quick down-up strum, creating a bit more drive rhythmically. The hammer-ons remain the same, as does the chord progression. In fact, refer to Fig. 2 for the complete chord progression, applying the following strumming variation to it.

Remember: all of these rhythms are completely interchangeable with one another.

Fig. 3

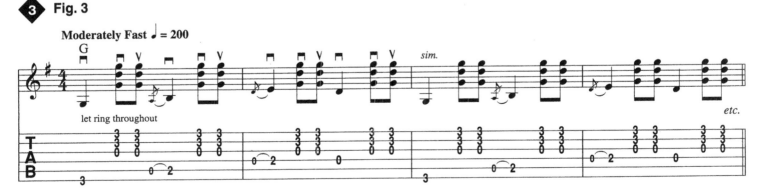

The Peavine Special

"The Peavine Special" is an example of *Travis picking*—a driving style that sounds almost like two guitarists playing at once. A staple of roots country, rockabilly, and modern country guitar, Travis picking sounds as fresh and immediate today as it did forty years ago on records like Elvis Presley's "That's Alright Mama" and "Mystery Train." The sound is produced by playing a short rhythmic figure using your fingers, and adding an alternating bass line simultaneously with your pick or thumb. Every guitarist should have a strong Travis groove in his or her bag of tricks.

This song is also based on a new progression, with some more advanced chord voicings. Here are some performance tips:

- Use a "classic" country right hand: flatpick, middle (m), and ring (a) fingers. When playing chords, your ring finger takes the highest note; your middle finger, the next highest.
- The foundation for each lick is the strong, alternating quarter-note bass line. Play it with flatpicked downstrokes. Be sure to mute the bass notes using the heel of your right hand so that you hear a percussive thump.
- Practice each lick slowly until you feel a rolling flow, then link them together as a progression.
- In measures 1-7, barre the A chord with your second finger. Just roll it over from the E7.
- In measure 9, use a fifth-fret half barre to hammer into A7. Follow this with a ring finger, seventh-fret half barre, to give you a quick D triad. Use this same move a whole step higher for the B7 lick in measure 17.
- Measures 19-20 feature a banjo roll on descending diatonic triads. Watch the right-hand fingering, and keep the bass notes alternating steadily.
- Use the bridge pickup on your guitar for more twang.

 Fig. 4

Chapter 2 Fingerstyle Acoustic

Fingerstyle acoustic playing has its roots in early blues. At first, blues guitarists used quarter-note ostinato bass notes to produce rhythms. Later on, they began to experiment with alternating bass notes, and accompaniment patterns began to develop. These patterns—alternating bass notes with one or two fingers on higher strings—eventually developed into the mainstays of today's folk styles. In this chapter, we will look at some popular and versatile fingerpicking patterns, putting them into progressions with other embellishments.

Four Basic Patterns

We'll begin with four basic fingerpicking patterns—these are some of the most commonly used in fingerstyle acoustic playing. The bass notes in each pattern are identical. The only difference is that the high notes are played in different combinations.

Fig. 1 shows the four patterns applied to an open-position D major chord (a four-string chord). Begin each pattern by just playing the bass notes to establish the rhythmic pulse. Then introduce the higher notes. Unless otherwise indicated, the notes with the stems pointed downward are played with the thumb (p), and the notes with the stems pointed upward are played with the fingers of your picking hand. For all of these examples, use your index (i) finger to play the second string and your middle finger (m) to play the first string.

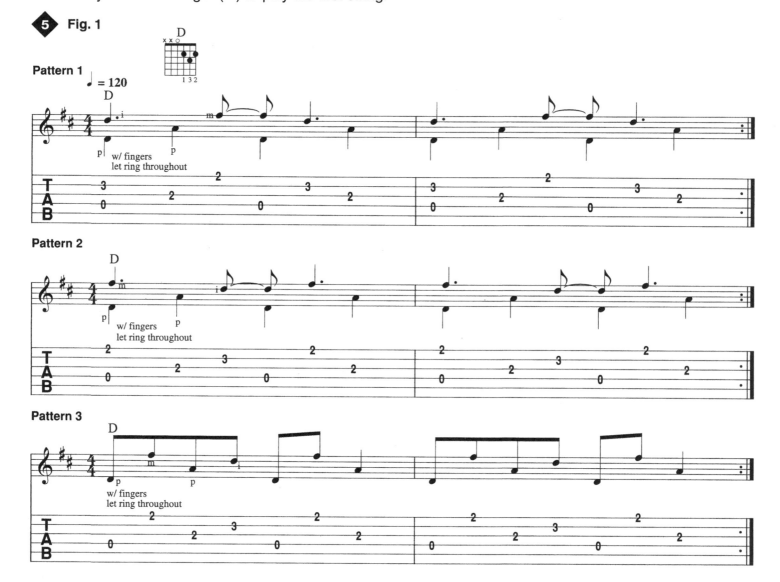

5 Fig. 1

Haymaker's Daughter

This is a short song that utilizes only four-string chords. Continue the alternating bass notes throughout. The triads on the top three strings provide some interesting sounds against the constant alternating bass—a common juxtaposition in fingerstyle acoustic playing. This song is written using only pattern 2. After learning it, play it using patterns 1, 3, and 4.

6 Fig. 2

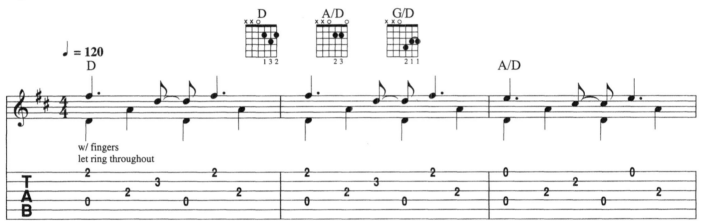

Reflections

"Relections" again uses only four-string chords and is written using pattern 2. Check out how it sounds if you play it using patterns 1, 3, or 4. The sus2 and sus4 chords are two popular embellishments in fingerstyle guitar and are introduced here. Endings 1 and 2 feature more "triads over bass notes" as well as a chord harmonic at the seventh fret. To play the harmonics, lightly barre the three strings indicated. Pluck the strings using your thumb, index, and middle fingers while simultaneously removing your barre from the strings. The resulting sound should be a harp-like chime.

 Fig. 3

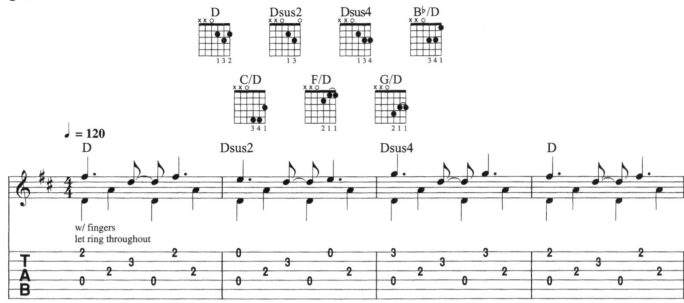

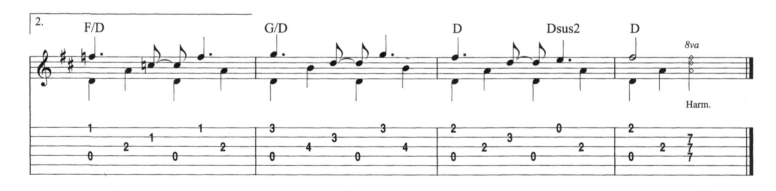

In the Meantime

"In the Meantime" uses the same four-string patterns but applied to larger, five-string chord fingerings. Notice that your thumb continues to play the alternating bass, but now it must skip across a string to do so. Don't forget to play it using all four fingerpicking patterns.

8 Fig. 4

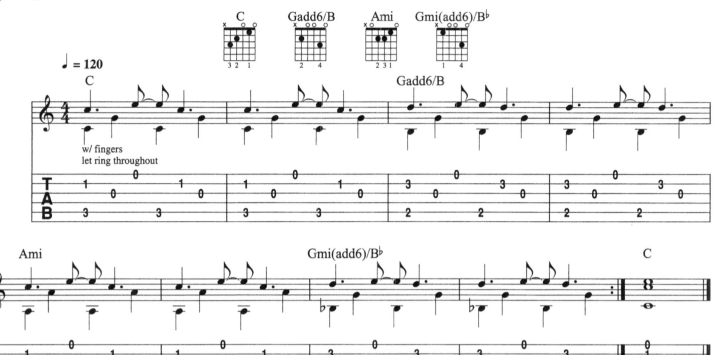

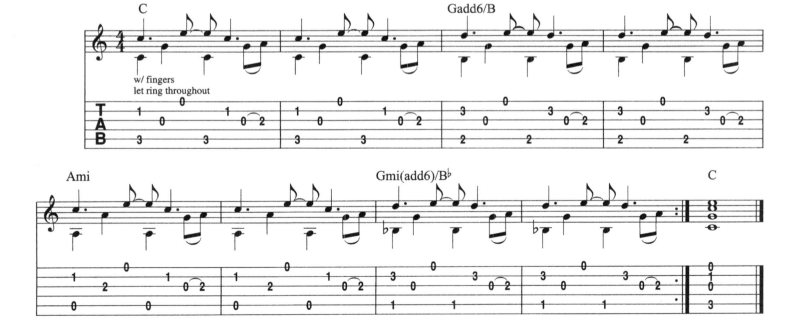

In the Meantime—Variation

Here is a variation on "In the Meantime" that replaces the bass note on beat 4 of each measure with a hammer-on. It can be tricky at first, but the pleasant chugging sound that it produces is well worth the practice time.

9 Fig. 5

Banish Misfortune

Here is a song that combines four-, five-, and six-string chord fingerings. Although it is written using pattern 1, don't forget to practice it in the other three patterns. Each pattern will give it an entirely different sound.

10 Fig. 6

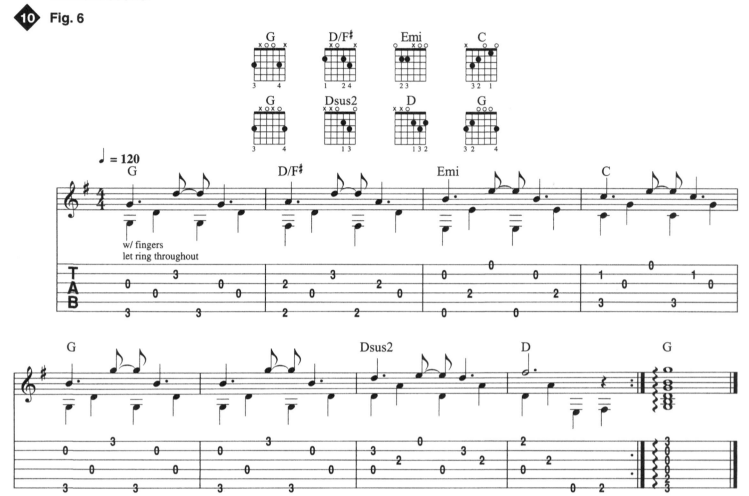

Waltz Delicioso

Every fingerstyle guitarist should be able to play in 3/4 time, because so many beautiful songs have been written in the waltz form. This next song in 3/4 incorporates four-, five-, and six-string chord fingerings, and features a descending bass line reminiscent of many great American folk songs. The right-hand fingerpicking pattern is distinctly different here: Begin with your thumb, then follow with your index (or first) finger, and your middle and ring fingers for the double stops (two notes played simultaneously).

11 Fig. 7

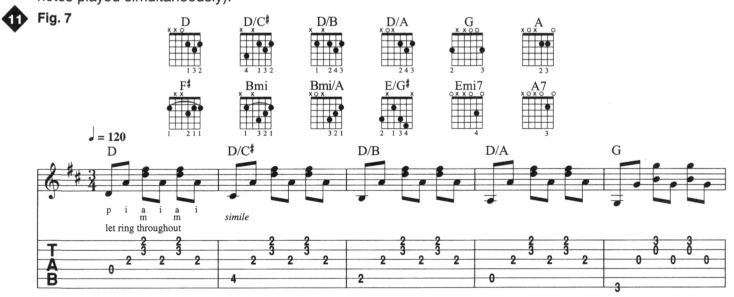

Fig Tree Blues

This next song is a classic 12-bar blues with a ragtime feel. It uses an alternating bass, which sounds best when the bass notes are muted using the heel of your picking hand (this is called *palm muting,* notated by P.M. between notation and tab staves). Play all of the bass notes (stems pointing down) with your thumb, and play the melody—which is more freestyle this time—with your index and middle fingers. This song is in the key of E and is played entirely in open position.

Pedal-Tone Riffs

Figs. 9 through 13 are bluesy riffs using an A *pedal tone*—a single note played in a steady rhythm, providing a continuous driving pulse. Fig. 9 is played in the fifth position. The idea is to create a quarter-note pulse using the bass notes and then play a syncopated rhythm over the top of it. Play the bass note with your thumb and the top notes using either your index and middle or your middle and ring fingers.

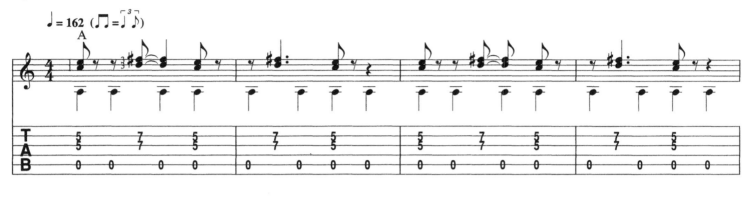

Figs. 10 through 13 are variations on a riff. Practice them slowly, and get the syncopation right. Gradually work them up to the desired tempo of 120 bpm. These short examples should be fun to play and can be repeated, interchanged, or used as a springboard to create other ideas.

14 **Fig. 10**   **Fig. 11**

Fig. 12   **Fig. 13**

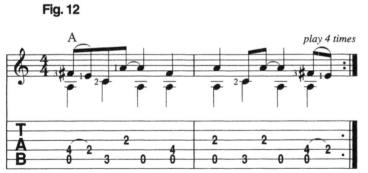

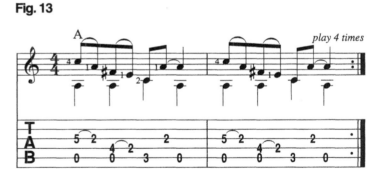

Chapter 3 Blues

The first aspect of blues to discuss is its musical form. Most often, the blues is based on twelve bars, or measures, which are repeated over and over. At the end of each twelve bars (called a chorus) is a turnaround, which is simply a short musical statement that points the listener back to the beginning. Although there are other blues forms, the 12-bar blues is by far the most common.

Blues is also played in several styles or feels, the two most popular being: 1) the shuffle, and 2) the straight eighth-note. The shuffle is a loping, forward-propelling feel that appears on virtually every blues album or CD that you can think of. The straight eighth-note feel, by contrast, is even, steady, and driving. It is a common blues feel and, because of its drive, has become the backbone of rock.

The Medium Shuffle

Our first example is a basic 12-bar blues shuffle. This is also known as the I–IV–V progression because the three chords that are played are dominant or seventh chords built on the first, fourth, and fifth degrees of the scale. It's shown here in the key of E, but of course it may be played in any key. The last measure contains the turnaround—this is typically the V7 chord approached from a half step above or below; in this case, from a half step above, or C5.

This is probably the most commonly played blues rhythm. It sounds best when:

- It is played using all downstrokes with your picking hand.
- It is muted using the heel of your picking hand close to the guitar bridge (P.M.).
- It is played staccato by lightly bouncing your fretting hand just after each pickstroke to achieve a "dat-dah, dat-dah, dat-dah, dat-dah" sound.

 Fig. 1

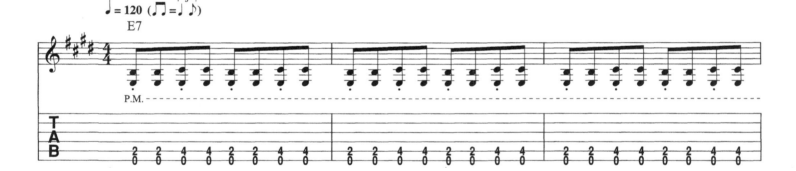

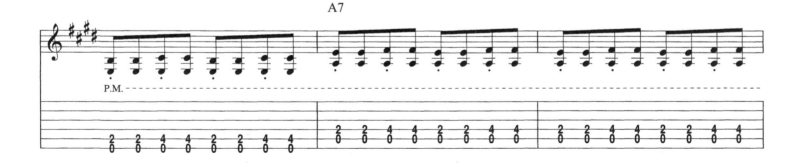

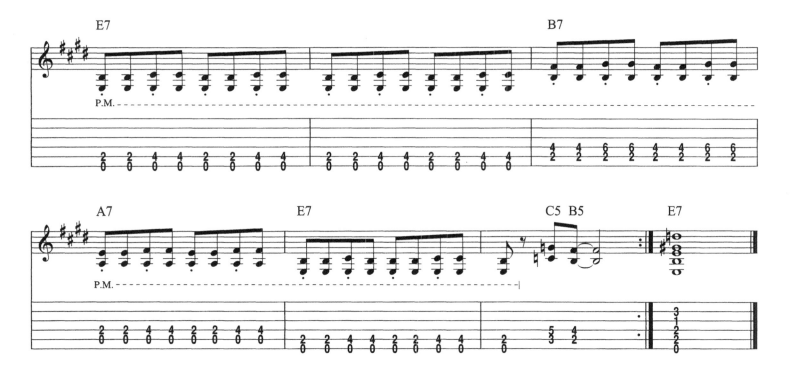

NOTE: Occasionally, in the 12-bar blues, the IV chord will appear in measure 2 and return to the I7 chord for measures 3 and 4. This variation is called the "quick change" form.

Variation—Chord Slide

This is another very popular and versatile rhythm. Notice that you never play on beat 1. This type of rhythm is called a work song or "axe" song. Slave workers would sing in the fields to pass the time—beat 1 was purposely left off the measure, and that became the beat on which the axe or similar tool fell; this would be a method of synchronizing the workers. It still stands today as a great approach to blues rhythm. To play it, fret each chord, play it on beat 2 of each measure, and then slide it down two frets. The chord should sound for the remainder of the measure.

 Fig. 2

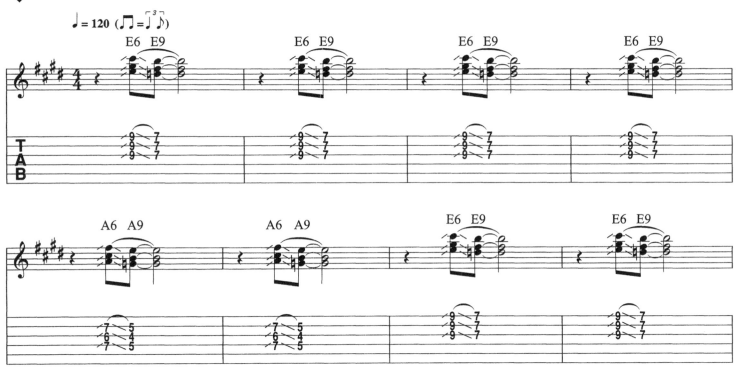

Straight Eighths Blues-Rock

Fig. 3 is a fairly simple one to play because it uses small first-position chords. You play the chords first and then play the pickup notes. The jump from chords to single notes and back to chords again might be tricky at first, but the reward of time spent mastering this one will be well worth it!

Notice that this uses a straight eighth-note feel, which gives it a rock edge. If you like, try it using a shuffle rhythm instead—this will give it a more laidback blues sound.

 Fig. 3

Variation—Seventh Chords

Fig. 4 is a variation of Fig. 5. All of the right-hand movement is the same except that there are more notes. Watch carefully because the F7 and G7 chords move up the fretboard to the sixth and eighth positions respectively. You'll first see this happen in the second half of measure 4.

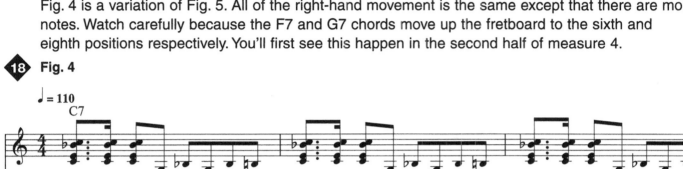

18 Fig. 4

Variation—Open Chords

Fig. 5 is in the key of E. It has always been one of my personal favorites. The strumming directions are indicated and should pose no problem. Be sure that you play each chord sharply and stop it from ringing immediately after it is sounded. This will ensure the percussive sound that this type of rhythm requires. Have fun.

 Fig. 5

Uptown Swing à la B. B. King

This rhythm requires no long explanation. It is simply a driving, killer rhythm that sounds great in medium to fast blues shuffles à la "Every Day I Have the Blues" by B.B. King. Watch the tempo on this one, as these type of upbeat rhythms tend to speed up if not checked.

 Fig. 6

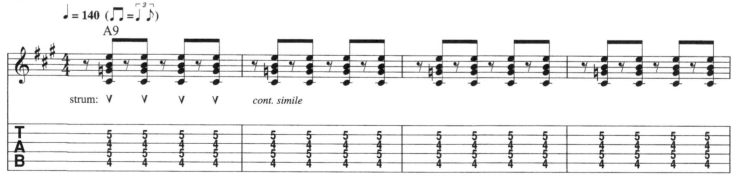

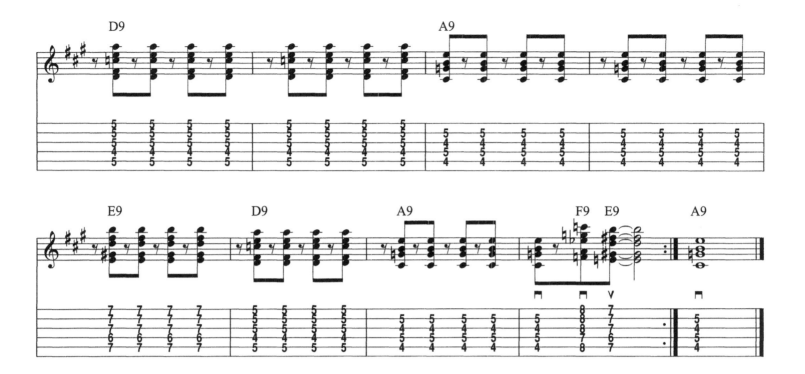

Variation—Horn Punch Rhythm

Fig. 7 is a horn punch rhythm for a blues shuffle at a faster tempo. Imagine a four-piece horn section playing together and driving B.B. King's band to a feverish pitch. The larger chord voicings give it a slick, uptown sound. Play this rhythm as short, brassy staccato stabs to get the desired effect. The turnaround is produced by playing a half-step slide from F9 to E9. Remember that a typical turnaround may be played by utilizing a half-step slide into the V7 chord from either above or below.

 Fig. 7

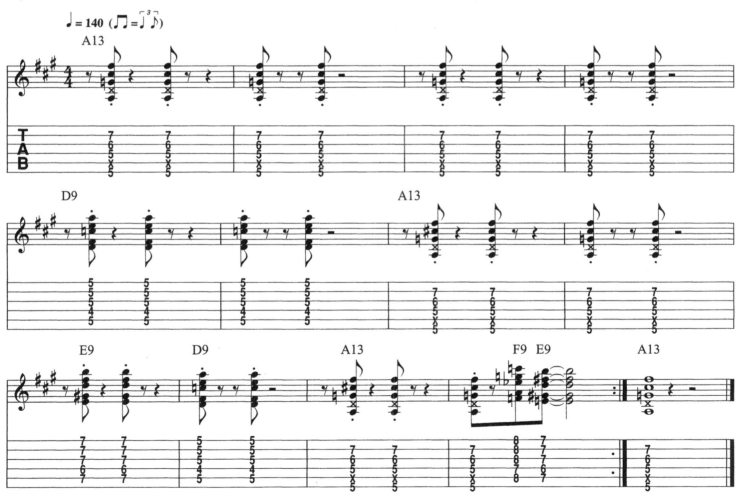

Rock music has come to encompass a variety of substyles—the early rock 'n' roll of the '50s, the classic rock of the '60s and '70s, the hard rock of the '70s and '80s, and the modern rock of the '90s.

Originally an offshoot of the blues, early rock favored the I–IV–V progression of 12-bar blues but played with a distinctly straight eighth-note feel. Gradually, the style expanded to encompass other forms and progressions, even borrowing liberally from other genres—country, Latin, jazz, etc. Today, just about anything goes. But the straight eighth-note still remains the most common feel of rock, and the I, IV, and V the most popular chords. This chapter contains several great and usable rock guitar rhythm ideas that span the decades from the '50s through the '90s.

Rock 'n' Roll

Fig. 1 is in the style of Chuck Berry, George Thorogood, Bob Seger, or Pat Travers. It's a 12-bar blues in the key of E—but played with a straight eighth-note feel. This is *the* rhythm that you would use if you were playing a basic three-chord blues/rock song. Even the Beatles relied on this pattern as the backbone for numerous hits.

This will sound best if you follow these suggestions:

- Dial in a crunch rhythm sound (not too much distortion).
- Use all downstrokes with your pick.
- Use your bridge pickup (if you have one).
- Use a heavy-gauge pick (.096-.114 mm).

22 **Fig. 1**

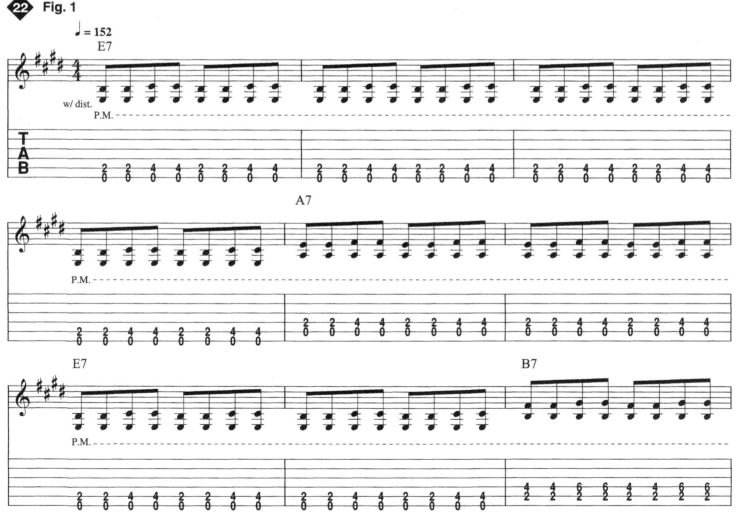

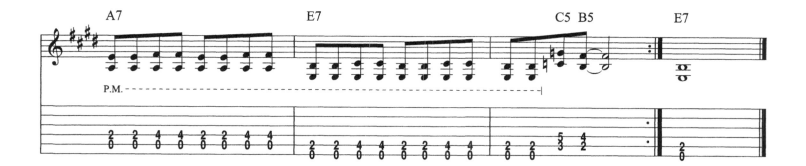

Fig. 2 is a variation of Fig. 1. It's another 12-bar blues, but played in the key of A with a somewhat heavier rock feel, á la Led Zeppelin. This is a classic rock rhythm guitar part and may be used for any number of songs. The feel is straight eighth-note, and it really drives. Notice the tasteful use of hammer-ons as well as the frequent anticipations on the "and" of beat 4 that carry into the next measure.

23 Fig. 2

Classic Rock

Fig. 3 is in the style of the Rolling Stones' guitarist Keith Richards. Keith has created such a signature sound that it is synonymous with the style of the Stones. He typically plays with only five guitar strings, removing the low sixth string. He then tunes his guitar to an open G chord (low to high: G–D–G–B–D). This tuning yields some unique chord voicings that feature the 5th of the chord in the bass.

For this example, we'll simulate this sound without changing our basic tuning. To do this requires some new voicings for old chords. In the first two measures, you will need to use your little finger to play the sixth string on the C and F/C chords. In measure 5, you will play basic familiar chords with the root note on the fifth string, using your little finger to play the sus4 on the second string—a Richards staple.

Notice again the rhythmic anticipations on the "and" of beat 4 in each measure; this is a favorite rhythmic concept in rock. For best results, play this loose and a bit sloppy—like Keith would.

 Fig. 3

Hard Rock

Fig. 4 is in the style of hard rock legends AC/DC. This is a great rock guitar rhythm and is played using only barre chords. The chord voicings are movable—to play this example in other keys, you simply find the fret on which the root tone of the first chord appears, and begin the progression there.

For best results:

- Dial in a nasty distorted tone.
- Pick using only downstrokes.

25 Fig. 4

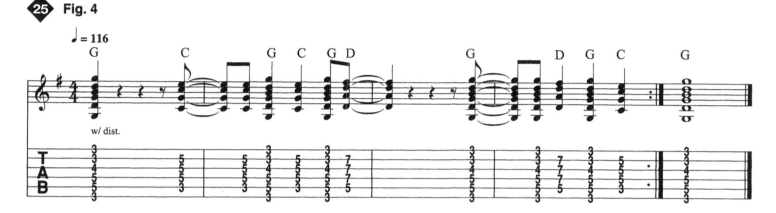

Fig. 5 is also in the style of AC/DC but showcases another facet of hard rock; it's in open position and based on an A minor riff. For best results, use alternate picking throughout, and a delay effect set for one repeat at approximately 150 milliseconds.

26 Fig. 5

Fig. 6 is a rhythm lick in the style of '80s rock guitar icon Eddie Van Halen. It's tricky, because you need to use your little finger to pull off from the fifth to the second fret and then jump way up to the eighth fret in the last measure to play the final slide. Be sure to check out the left-hand fingerings. Executing these jumps wouldn't necessarily be difficult except that the tempo of this lick is very fast.

For best results:

- Dial in a crunchy distortion.
- Turn up the treble on your amp to one number higher than you normally play.
- Turn up the volume on your amp to "arena rock."

Modern Rock

Modern rock has as one of its unique sounds the frequent occurrence of oblique, somewhat illogical chord progressions. Here is a good example of this. Fig. 7 is a contemporary rhythm in the style of Nirvana, Dishwalla, or Alanis Morrisette. For this example, play only power chords, and don't include any thirds in the chords. Notice the "sus2" chords in the second half. These are essentially power chords with the addition of the second degree on top. They're a popular substitute for major and minor chords in rock because they don't contain a third degree and therefore sound ambiguous and not too "pretty."

For best results:

- Dial in a crunch rhythm sound.
- Play a bit loosely, with a rough, angst feel.
- Use a heavy-gauge pick (.096-.114 mm).

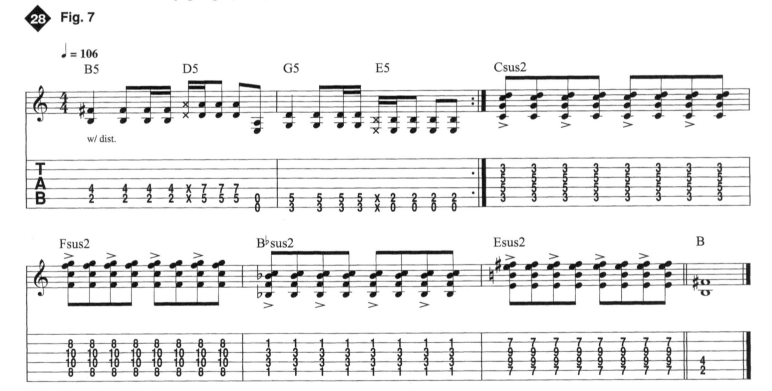

This example is more of a singer/songwriter type of chord progression in the style of Sheryl Crow. Begin by barring the seventh fret with your index finger. Each hammer-on in the first four measures is played on string 3 using your little finger. The D, G, Bm, and C chords in the last four measures are arpeggiated using your pick. Watch the fingering in this section, or you'll get tangled up.

For the best sound:

- Use your bridge pickup.
- Dial in your amp sound with the reverb and treble set approximately one number higher than where you usually play.
- Use a delay set for one repeat at 200-220 milliseconds.

 Fig. 8

Here's a great acoustic guitar rhythm, á la Natalie Imbruglia, that uses barre chords. The chord voicings used are pictured as fretboard diagrams. The actual rhythm is shown in measure 1 and is used throughout the example.

For the best sound:

- Use an acoustic guitar.
- Keep your picking hand moving evenly, in a steady up-and-down motion.
- Use a thin to medium-thickness pick.

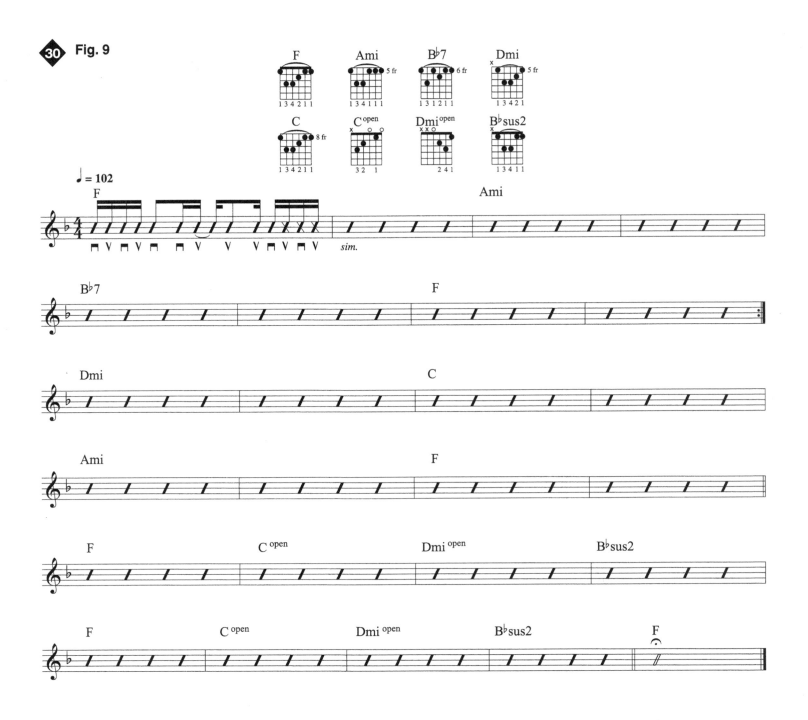

Here's one more acoustic example, this one in the style of Third Eye Blind. I've included it because it features some interesting chords. Watch the chord block diagrams for the fingerings. Pay close attention to the pick direction markings, and the rhythm will have a nice flow. Play the Dadd9add4/A chord by simply moving the fingering of the C chord up two frets.

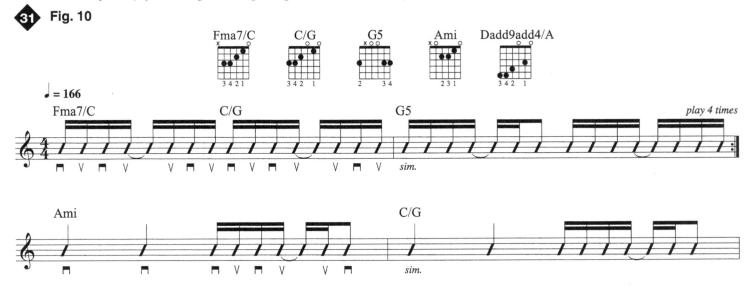

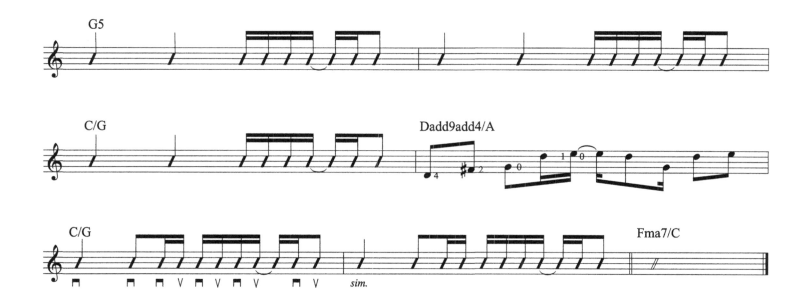

Chapter 5 — Latin / Brazilian

Latin music is an extremely rhythmic style, oriented toward dance. Although it has been played throughout South and Latin America, it has entered into the mainstream of American pop music through the success of bands like Santana and the Miami Sound Machine featuring Gloria Estefan.

Samba Clave

Most Latin rhythm is based on what is called the *samba clave* rhythm. Fig. 1 demonstrates the samba clave in its basic form. Notice that this is essentially a two-measure rhythm, applied to a series of chords. If you need to play two measures of a chord, the pattern poses no problem; however, a small change is necessary if the chord progression changes every measure. If that happens—as it does in measure 5 below—the chord in the second measure of the pattern is anticipated by playing it on the last eighth note of the previous measure. By the way, this pattern can be played with a pick; however, I'm using my thumb and fingers in unison here, playing four-note chord voicings.

32 Fig. 1

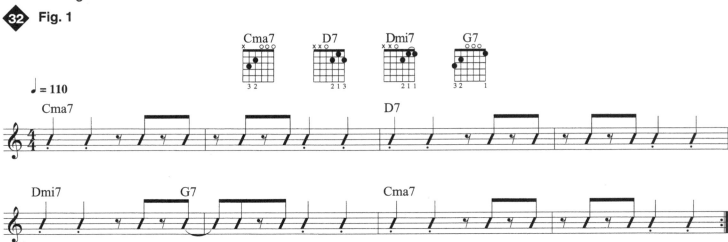

Clave Variations

Figs. 2, 3, 4, and 5 are popular variations of the basic clave rhythm. If the song being played falls into the category of bossa nova, samba, or Latin rock, any of the rhythms in Figures 1 through 5 may be played on the chord progression.

33 Fig. 2   Fig. 3

Fig. 4   Fig. 5

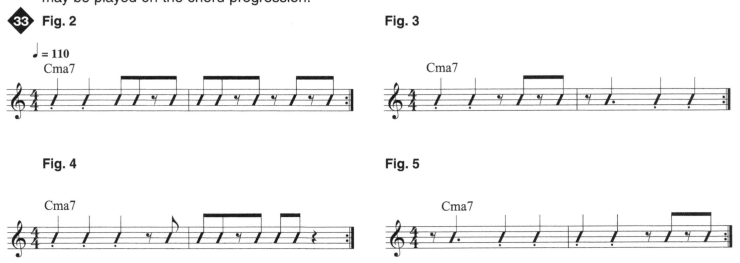

Another Progression

Here's another popular Latin rhythm, again two measures in length. Notice this time, however, there are two chords per measure. This was a popular rhythm for guitarist Carlos Santana. I use a pick for this one.

Fig. 6

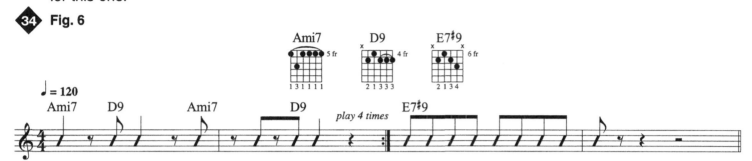

Thumb-and-Finger Patterns

Figures 7 through 10 are played using your thumb and fingers in alternation. The syncopation is tricky and may require some practice. The rule for playing these examples is to play the root or tonic note of the chord with your thumb (on the notes where the stem points downward) and pluck the remainder of the chord (up to three notes) using your index, middle, and ring fingers simultaneously.

Fig. 7   **Fig. 8**

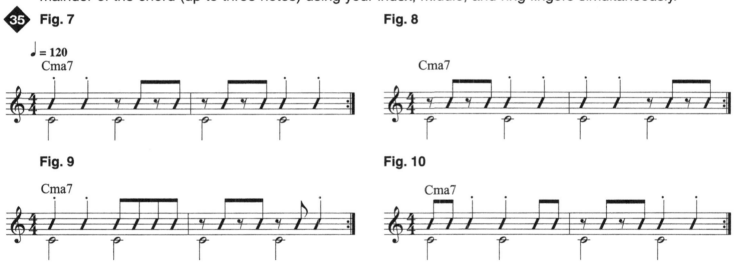

Fig. 9   **Fig. 10**

Variation—Alternating Bass

A more authentic variation may be played by alternating bass notes with your thumb between the root and fifth of each chord. Fig. 11 is a variation of Fig. 7 but this time with an alternating bass note pattern. I've also added some contemporary chord voicings that exemplify the Latin guitar sound. The bass notes are played on beats 1 and 3, which helps center the syncopated rhythms.

NOTE: In Figures 11 and 12, the alternating bass note is shown in parentheses on the fretboard diagrams.

Fig. 11

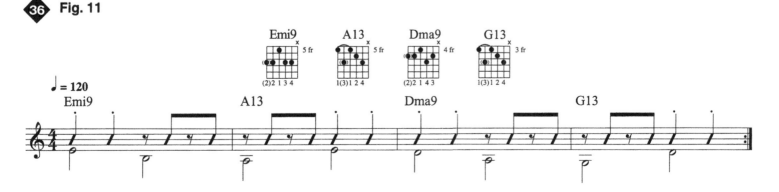

Fig. 12 is rhythmically identical to Fig. 8. This time, however, with alternating bass notes. The chord voicings are typical of Latin guitar music.

Fig. 12

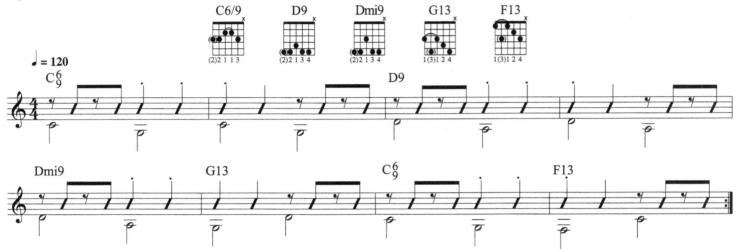

Chapter 6 — Jazz & Swing

Rhythm guitar in jazz and swing music is less about hard-driving, continuous rhythm and more about sparsely punctuating the music with well-placed chords or short fills. The art of accompaniment, or "comping" as it is called in this style of music, is, of course, knowing when to play and when not to.

Four-to-the-Bar

First let's talk about the type of rhythm that most of us are familiar with in regards to jazz: the "four-to-the-bar" style of playing. This type of rhythm was made famous by guitarist Freddie Green during his time with the Count Basie Orchestra. The chord shapes are generally three- or four-note, and the concept is to play steady chords on every beat of the music, regarding the guitar as almost more of a percussive instrument than a melodic one.

Fig. 1 demonstrates this technique using a standard 12-bar jazz-blues chord progression. For the best sound:

- Use the neck pickup for a clean, somewhat dark tone.
- Use a stiff pick, and strum fairly hard.
- Pick using all downstrokes.
- Mute all unwanted strings with your picking hand.

38 Fig. 1

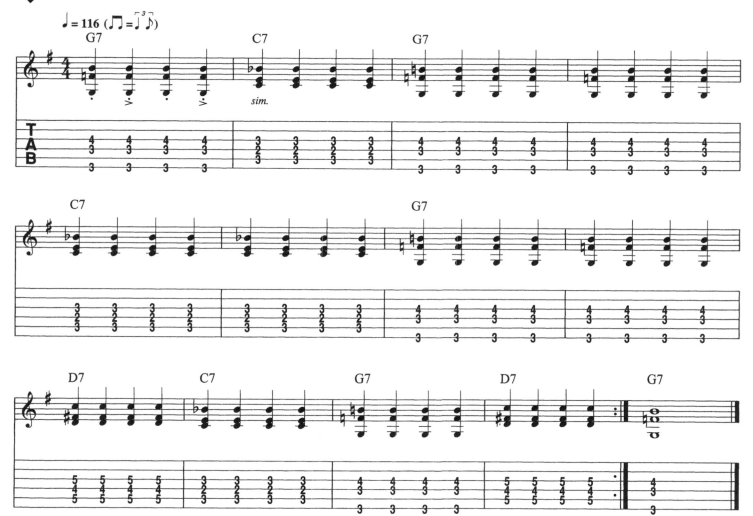

Walking Bass

This next example is again written for a standard 12-bar blues progression. It is called walking bass. For this rhythm, the bass notes will be played as uninterrupted quarter notes, four to each measure. Chord fragments that suggest the chord movement will be added at certain places in each measure; this happens most frequently on the upbeat of beats 1 and/or 3 of each measure. The key of F was chosen for this example because of the availability of the low register of the guitar.

Fig. 2 sounds best when:

- A pick is used for all of the bass notes, and fingers are extended to grab the double stops.
- A dark, clean sound is dialed in.
- A heavy pick is used.
- All of the bass notes are played using downstrokes, and double stops are played with the fingers.
- A steady, even pulse is created, and all bass notes and double stops are played at equal volume.

39 **Fig. 2**

36

Turnarounds

Turnarounds, as the name implies, are musical ways of returning a piece of music back to its beginning. The turnaround is found at the end of a piece of music—usually, it's four chords occupying either one or two beats each, appearing during the last one or two measures of a song or progression. Turnarounds are typically made up of the I, VImi, IImi, and V7 chords of the key of whatever song you are playing.

Fig. 3 is our most basic turnaround, played in the "four-to-the-bar" style. Notice that each chord here has only its most essential notes—the tonic, the third, and the seventh. This turnaround would fit well with the progression in Fig. 1; just substitute it for the last two measures before the repeat. Fig. 4 is a variation on Fig. 3, which substitutes E♭7/B♭ for the A7 chord. This, too, would work well as a turnaround for Fig. 1. Figures 5 and 6 are more jazz-like, due to the use of the major tonic, G or Gma7, instead of the dominant seventh, G7. These would work well in a more major, upbeat jazz progression. Fig. 7 returns to the dominant seventh sound but has an extended quality, due to the thirteenth chords used.

All of the chords in these examples are movable and should be transposed to all keys. Doing this will provide you with a repertoire of turnarounds that may be used in any key in which you are required to play. Remember: Turnarounds are more or less interchangeable.

NOTE: Turnarounds are usually played only once at the end of a song; however, for practice, the following turnarounds are each played here four times.

Fig. 3

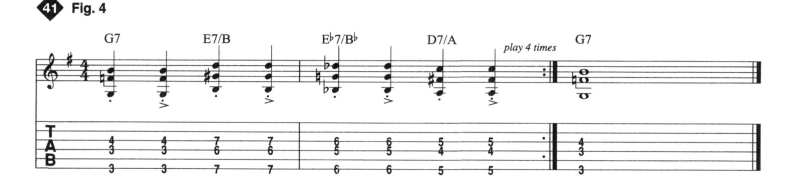

Fig. 4

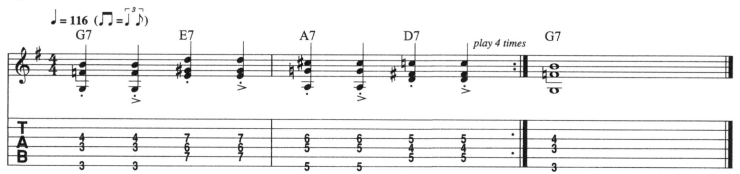

Fig. 5

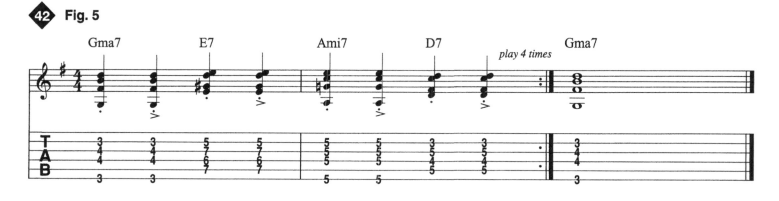

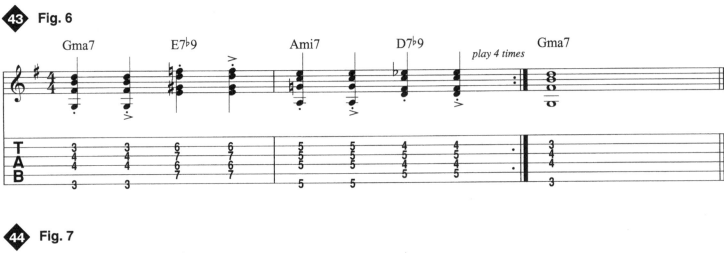

43 **Fig. 6**

44 **Fig. 7**

II-V7-I-IV Progressions

Now let's return to our earlier idea of comping, or sparsely punctuating a song rhythmically, which is more typical in standard jazz guitar. This is done so that the soloist isn't restricted rhythmically. Here are four examples of jazz/swing-type rhythms with chord voicings typically used in jazz. Notice that the chords sound richer than basic guitar chords; this is due to the addition of chord extensions and alterations. The progression that I've chosen to work with is a standard in jazz music. It's called the II–V7–I–IV progression. This combination of chords appears more often in jazz music than any other progression.

Fig. 8 is in the key of G major. The chords are straightforward, as are the rhythms. The rhythmic pulse is provided by the bass and/or the drums so, as a guitarist, you need only punctuate the rhythm. Fig. 9 is in the key of C major. Between Figs. 8 and 9, there are enough chords to play this progression in any key. Each of the chords are movable shapes, so to practice in different keys, all you need to do is find the root, or tonic (circled), and build each chord around it.

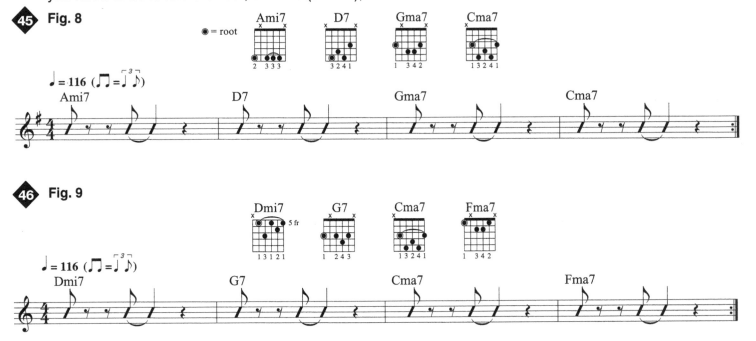

45 **Fig. 8**

46 **Fig. 9**

Figs. 10 and 11 are merely variations of Fig. 8 and may be used interchangeably. Fig. 10 uses smaller shapes and provides a melodic line in the top voices of the chords. Fig. 11 is another variation of the same progression and uses additional chord voicings. Notice how the chords in measures 2 and 4 are anticipated (played on the upbeat of beat 4). This is standard practice in this style and may be used anytime. Again, all of these chords are movable and should eventually be transposed to all keys.

 Fig. 10

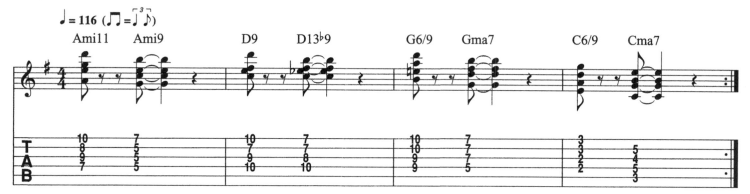

 Fig. 11

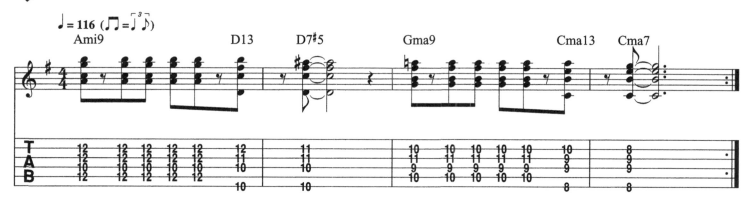

Chapter 7 Funk

Funk is a pure form of rhythm guitar. It makes you think of your six-string as a percussion instrument—like a drum kit. When you're playing funk, you have to stay focused, laying down a steady, uninterrupted flow of rhythm that provides the forward momentum and, sometimes, a song's essential guitar hook.

Think of funk in two categories: original funk (before 1975) and modern funk (after 1975). The guitar parts in original funk (à la James Brown, Tower of Power, Kool & the Gang) use larger chord forms and are generally a bit busier rhythmically. Modern funk (à la Michael Jackson, Prince) features sparser rhythms and chord fragments of two or three notes. Single-note funk rhythms, known as "bubble" or "skank" parts, are also typical. Both styles should be part of every rhythm guitarist's vocabulary.

The Sixteenth-Note Scratch

As a general rule, funk music is based on a sixteenth-note subdivision: Each measure is divided into sixteen equal parts, four parts per beat. These sixteenths can be played straight or they can be played with a swing feel, as they are in these examples. The best way to get a handle on this subdivision is with a simple picking exercise.

Fig. 1 gets you started. Set the metronome at about 50 bpm to start. Using steady up-down strumming, play the E9 chord at the beginning of each beat, and scratch the next three sixteenth notes by loosening your grip on the chord. (Gradually, work up to the 90 bpm tempo indicated.)

For me, a large, medium-gauge pick with a little flex (about .90 mm) works best. Hold the pick loosely, and strum with a relaxed wrist. Try this: keep your picking hand open and your fingers extended—this provides a counterweight that helps keep the rhythm even. The real key is to keep the picking hand strumming the sixteenth-note rhythm, whether the notes are played, scratched (muted), or ghosted (not sounded).

For an authentic funk sound, dial in an ultra-clean tone with lots of treble—on many guitars, you'll use only the bridge pickup. This sound is very "up front," so it's important to pick precisely and stay on top of the time.

 Fig. 1

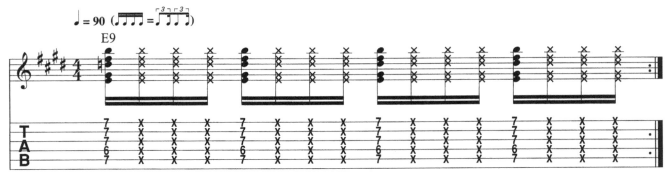

Classic Licks

Now let's get funky. Fig. 2A is a mainstay funk riff in the James Brown style. The third beat is ghosted: Let the dotted eighth-note rhythm ring, and continue the strumming motion by floating the pick just above the strings for the second and third sixteenths, then catch the last sixteenth on the upswing. Fig. 2B is straightforward. To make it a bit easier to play, I've eliminated the bass notes from the chords.

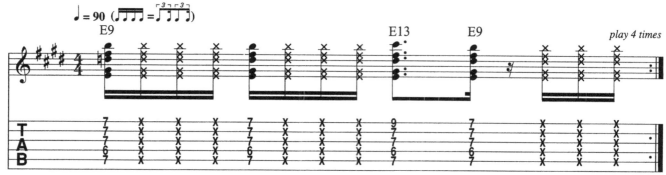

50 **Fig. 2A**

51 **Fig. 2B**

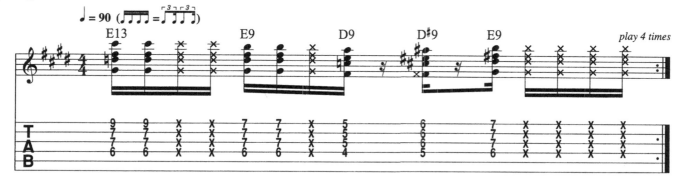

Fig. 3 is a classic lick à la Sly. The first measure uses *skank technique:* Strum three strings for every note, but sound only the string in the middle, muting the strings above and below with the fretting hand—use your thumb to mute the low E string.

The second measure requires a half-step slide. This is a bit tricky. The second chord of the slide, E9, is ghosted—your picking hand floats just above the strings and strums down, then catches the next sixteenth note on the upswing. Scratch the muted strings aggressively throughout.

52 **Fig. 3**

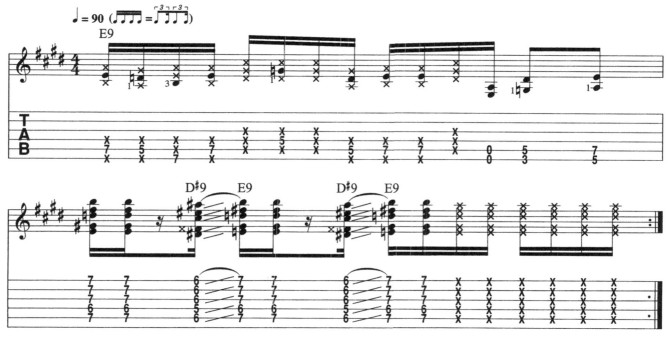

Fig. 4 is another James Brown groove. This time, the slide move starts on the downbeat, so your right hand floats on the up cycle of the slide (the second sixteenth note) while the left hand articulates the notes.

Fig. 4

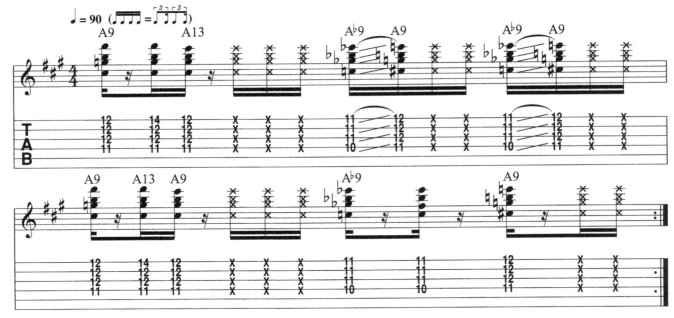

Fig. 5 is reminiscent of Earth, Wind & Fire. Scratch across all six strings, and really pronounce the rhythm. This time, strum both chords in the half-step slide to keep the rhythm flowing.

Fig. 5

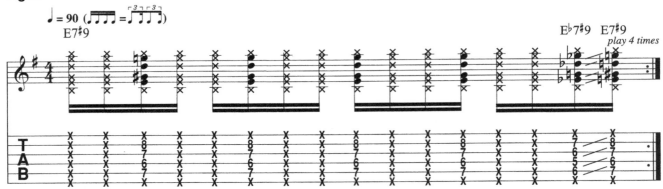

Fig. 6 is a funk-rock lick. The movement within the chord adds a suspended fourth to a dominant seventh chord. Start by scratching lightly on all six strings; as you get better, cut the scratches and float these notes.

Fig. 6

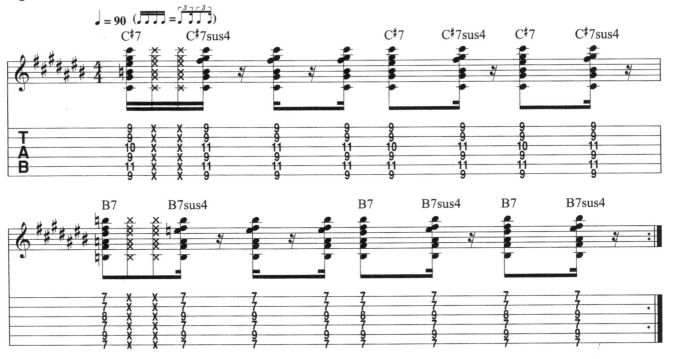

Fig. 7 evokes the riff in Prince's "1999." The idea here is to maintain an uninterrupted flow of rhythm while scratching very lightly across the top three strings so these notes don't jump out. The single notes in measure 2 are played skank style: Attack the single notes aggressively while muting the two adjacent strings—picking all three strings together creates a powerful effect. This technique is tricky and will take some practice.

Fig. 7

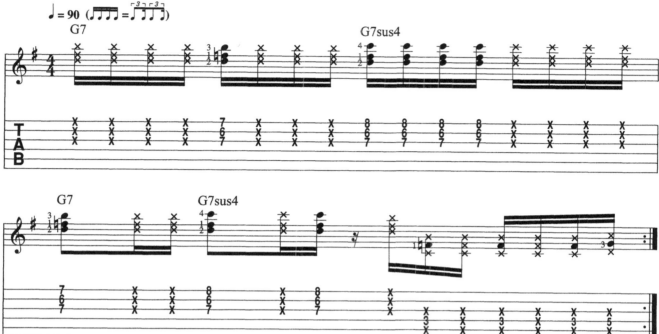

Skank and Bubble

Figs. 8 and 9 are both skank riffs, the first in the style of Nile Rodgers, the second in the style of the Isley Brothers. Go for an aggressive, percussive sound here.

Fig. 8

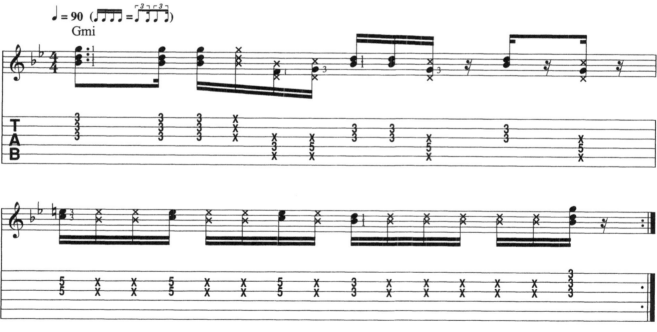

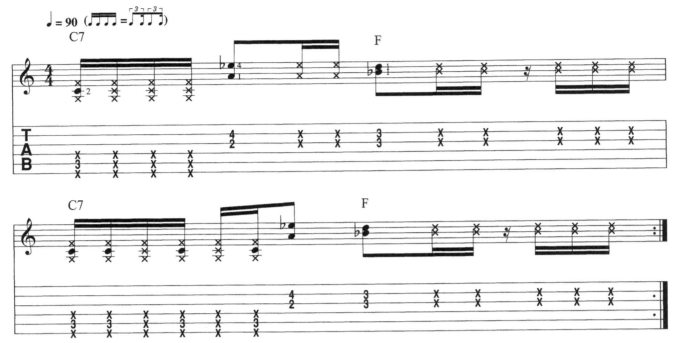

The next two licks are modern funk, which means smaller chord fragments and unusual intervals. Fig. 10 is built on stacked fourths. You'll probably have to practice this one very slowly until you can feel the rhythm. The phrasing is not typical, but once you master it, the sound is great. Fig. 11 is typical Prince. Compare these sparse, edgy lines with older riffs, and you'll see how funk guitar has evolved.

59 Fig. 10

60 Fig. 11

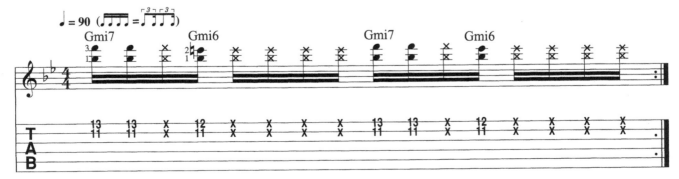

Fig. 12 is a muted single-note line, a bubble part in the style of Paul Jackson, Jr., as played on Michael Jackson's "Wanna Be Startin' Something." Play it on strings 1 and 2, muting them throughout with the heel of your picking hand.

Fig. 12

Based on Chaka Khan's "Have a Good Time," Fig. 13 is an aggressive skank line combined with double-stop chord fragments. Mute the strings on both sides of the single-note skank line with your fretting hand, and scratch it good and loud. The double stop in measure 2 is part of a minor sixth chord, a common sound in recent funk guitar.

Fig. 13

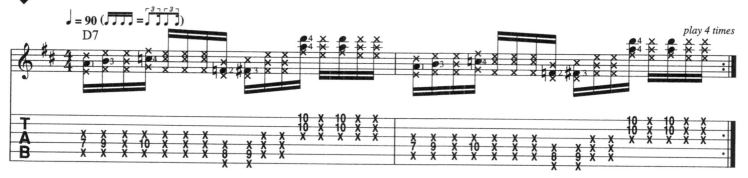

Fig. 14, in the tradition of the Staple Singers and the Meters, is a beautiful, long line that moves down the length of the fretboard. Its unique sound comes from the use of the major pentatonic scale, which gives it a gospel vibe. Play it with a mellow tone, scratch lightly to mark the time, and float your pick during the tied eighth notes. The last sixteenth-note scratch should provide enough time to jump back up to the ninth position.

Fig. 14

Fig. 15 is an example of "bubble picking" in the style of one of my all-time favorites, '80s studio great Lee Ritenour. Use your pick on string 4, and alternate with your middle finger on string 3. Mute the strings at the bridge with the heel of your picking hand. This one uses the two funkiest degrees in any chord, the 3rd and 7th. In measure 1, the 7th is on string 4, and the 3rd is on string 3. To play measure 2, just move the shape down one fret. Now it's F7, with the 3rd on string 4 and the 7th on string 3.

64 Fig. 15

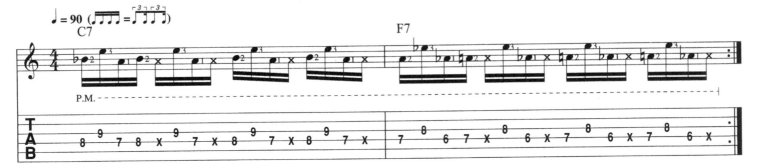

Fig. 16 is a riff my students always love. It's got a lot of ideas in it. The sixth intervals in measure 1 are played on strings 4 and 2. Mute the third string with your third finger. As with all these examples, keep the picking-hand motion uninterrupted. The end of the phrase loops around to the beginning with the last note tied to the first note. Have fun!

65 Fig. 16

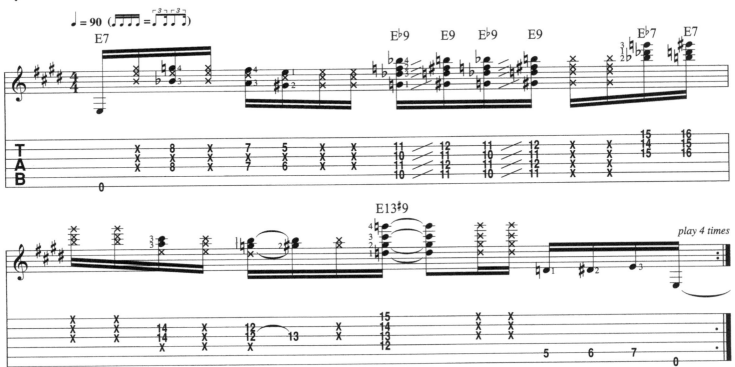

About the Author

Steve Trovato is currently an instructor in the Studio Jazz Guitar Department at the University of Southern California. He has authored over 20 instructional books, and is a regular contributor to *Guitar Player, GuitarOne, Axe, Guitar Club,* and *Guitar World* magazines. In addition to his teaching career, Steve maintains a busy performing and recording schedule. He has toured extensively in North America, Asia, and Europe, playing alongside such players as Robben Ford, Scott Henderson, Albert Collins, Jerry Donahue, Norman Brown, and Jeff Berlin.

MUSICIANS INSTITUTE PRESS is the official series of Southern California's renowned music school, Musicians Institute. MI instructors, some of the finest musicians in the world, share their vast knowledge and experience with you – no matter what your current level. For guitar, bass, drums, vocals, and keyboards, MI Press offers the finest music curriculum for higher learning through a variety of series:

ESSENTIAL CONCEPTS
Designed from MI core curriculum programs.

MASTER CLASS
Designed from MI elective courses.

PRIVATE LESSONS
Tackle a variety of topics "one-on one" with MI faculty instructors.

GUITAR

Acoustic Artistry
by Evan Hirschelman • **Private Lessons**
00695922 Book/Online Audio $24.99

Advanced Scale Concepts & Licks for Guitar
by Jean Marc Belkadi • **Private Lessons**
00695298 Book/CD Pack $22.99

All-in-One Guitar Soloing Course
by Daniel Gilbert & Beth Marlis
00217709 Book/Online Media $29.99

Blues/Rock Soloing for Guitar
by Robert Calva • **Private Lessons**
00695680 Book/Online Audio $22.99

Blues Guitar Soloing
by Keith Wyatt • **Master Class**
00695132 Book/Online Audio $29.99

Blues Rhythm Guitar
by Keith Wyatt • **Master Class**
00695131 Book/Online Audio $22.99

Dean Brown
00696002 DVD $29.95

Chord Progressions for Guitar
by Tom Kolb • **Private Lessons**
00695664 Book/Online Audio $19.99

Chord Tone Soloing
by Barrett Tagliarino • **Private Lessons**
00695855 Book/Online Audio $27.99

Chord-Melody Guitar
by Bruce Buckingham • **Private Lessons**
00695646 Book/Online Audio $22.99

Classical & Fingerstyle Guitar Techniques
by David Oakes • **Master Class**
00695171 Book/Online Audio $22.99

Classical Themes for Electric Guitar
by Jean Marc Belkadi • **Private Lessons**
00695806 Book/CD Pack $15.99

Country Guitar
by Al Bonhomme • **Master Class**
00695661 Book/Online Audio $22.99

Essential Rhythm Guitar
by Steve Trovato • **Private Lessons**
00695181 Book/CD Pack $16.99

Exotic Scales & Licks for Electric Guitar
by Jean Marc Belkadi • **Private Lessons**
00695860 Book/CD Pack $19.99

Funk Guitar
by Ross Bolton • **Private Lessons**
00695419 Book/Online Audio $17.99

Guitar Basics
by Bruce Buckingham • **Private Lessons**
00695134 Book/Online Audio $19.99

Guitar Fretboard Workbook
by Barrett Tagliarino • **Essential Concepts**
00695712 .... $22.99

Guitar Hanon
by Peter Deneff • **Private Lessons**
00695321 .... $17.99

Guitar Lick•tionary
by Dave Hill • **Private Lessons**
00695482 Book/CD Pack $22.99

Guitar Soloing
by Dan Gilbert & Beth Marlis • **Essential Concepts**
00695190 Book/Online Audio $24.99

Harmonics
by Jamie Findlay • **Private Lessons**
00695169 Book/CD Pack $16.99

Harmony & Theory
by Keith Wyatt & Carl Schroeder • **Essential Concepts**
00695161 .... $24.99

Introduction to Jazz Guitar Soloing
by Joe Elliott • **Master Class**
00695406 Book/Online Audio $24.99

Jazz Guitar Chord System
by Scott Henderson • **Private Lessons**
00695291 .... $14.99

Jazz Guitar Improvisation
by Sid Jacobs • **Master Class**
00217711 Book/Online Media $19.99

Jazz, Rock & Funk Guitar
by Dean Brown • **Private Lessons**
00217690 Book/Online Media $19.99

Latin Guitar
by Bruce Buckingham • **Master Class**
00695379 Book/Online Audio $19.99

Lead Sheet Bible
by Robin Randall & Janice Peterson • **Private Lessons**
00695130 Book/Online Audio $24.99

Liquid Legato
by Allen Hinds • **Private Lessons**
00696656 Book/Online Audio $17.99

Modern Jazz Concepts for Guitar
by Sid Jacobs • **Master Class**
00695711 Book/CD Pack $19.99

Modern Rock Rhythm Guitar
by Danny Gill • **Private Lessons**
00695682 Book/Online Audio $22.99

Modes for Guitar
by Tom Kolb • **Private Lessons**
00695555 Book/Online Audio $19.99

Music Reading for Guitar
by David Oakes • **Essential Concepts**
00695192 .... $24.99

Outside Guitar Licks
by Jean Marc Belkadi • **Private Lessons**
00695697 Book/CD Pack $16.99

Power Plucking
by Dale Turner • **Private Lesson**
00695962 Book/CD Pack $19.95

Progressive Tapping Licks
by Jean Marc Belkadi • **Private Lessons**
00695748 Book/CD Pack $19.99

Rhythm Guitar
by Bruce Buckingham & Eric Paschal • **Essential Concepts**
00695188 Book $22.99
00114559 Book/Online Audio $27.99
00695909 DVD $19.95

Rhythmic Lead Guitar
by Barrett Tagliarino • **Private Lessons**
00110263 Book/Online Audio $22.99

Rock Lead Basics
by Nick Nolan & Danny Gill • **Master Class**
00695144 Book/Online Audio $19.99

Rock Lead Performance
by Nick Nolan & Danny Gill • **Master Class**
00695278 Book/Online Audio $19.99

Rock Lead Techniques
by Nick Nolan & Danny Gill • **Master Class**
00695146 Book/Online Audio $19.99

Shred Guitar
by Greg Harrison • **Master Class**
00695977 Book/Online Audio $24.99

Solo Slap Guitar
by Jude Gold • **Master Class**
00139556 Book/Online Video.............. $24.99

Technique Exercises for Guitar
by Jean Marc Belkadi • **Private Lessons**
00695913 Book/CD Pack $17.99

Texas Blues Guitar
by Robert Calva • **Private Lessons**
00695340 Book/Online Audio $19.99

Ultimate Guitar Technique
by Bill LaFleur • **Private Lessons**
00695863 Book/Online Audio $24.99

Prices, contents, and availability subject to change without notice.

7777 W. BLUEMOUND RD. P.O. BOX 13819 MILWAUKEE, WI 53213

www.halleonard.com